T0059218

THE BEST OF JACK BRUCE

BASS TAB EDITION

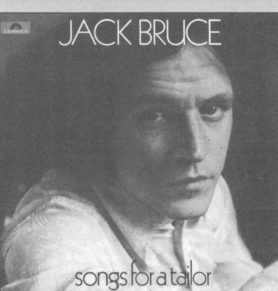

Alfred Music Publishing Co., Inc.
16320 Roscoe Blvd., Suite 100
P.O. Box 10003
Van Nuys, CA 91410-0003
alfred.com

ISBN-10: 0-7390-5901-7
ISBN-13: 978-0-7390-5901-2

CONTENTS

DESERTED CITIES OF THE HEART

Moderately ♩ = 124

Words and Music by
JACK BRUCE and PETE BROWN

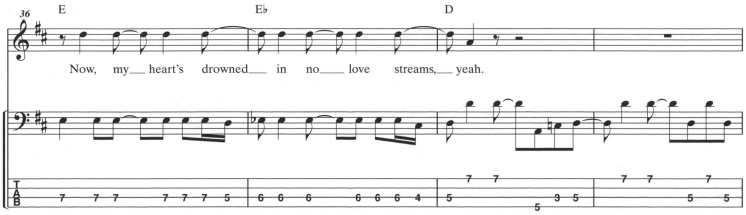

To Coda ⊕

Deserted Cities of the Heart - 5 - 3

Now, my___ heart's drowned_____ in no love streams, yeah._____

Guitar Solo:

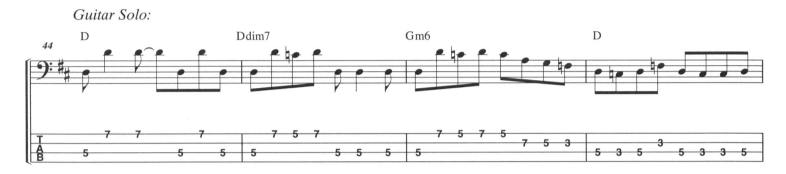

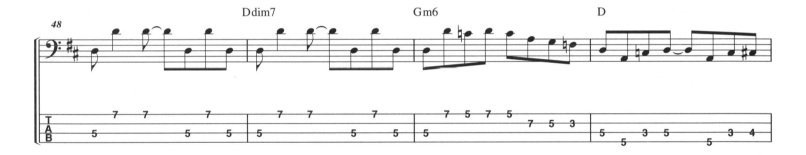

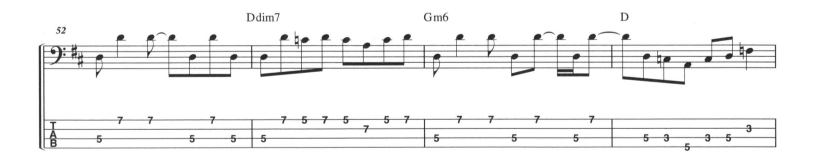

D.S. %̸ al Coda

Coda

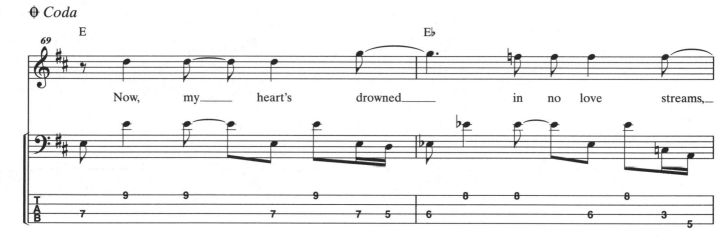

Now, my___ heart's drowned___ in no love streams,___

___ yeah. Now, my___ heart's drowned___

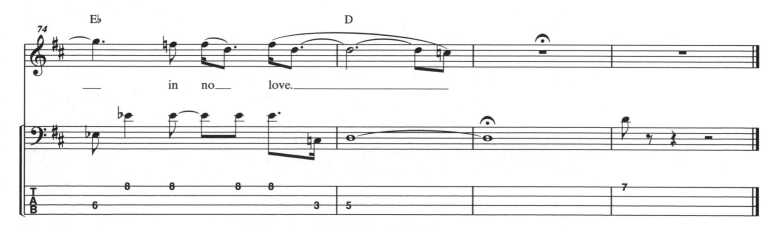

___ in no___ love.___

DANCE THE NIGHT AWAY

Words and Music by
JACK BRUCE and PETE BROWN

*Bass Gtr. simile on repeats.

Dance the Night Away - 4 - 1

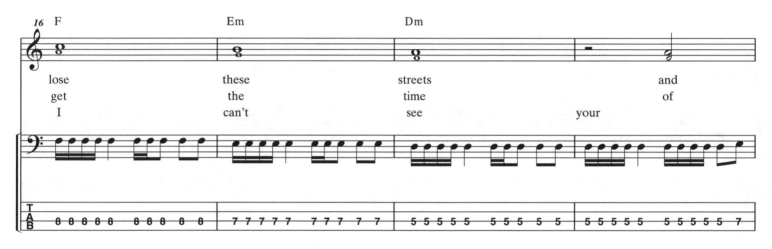

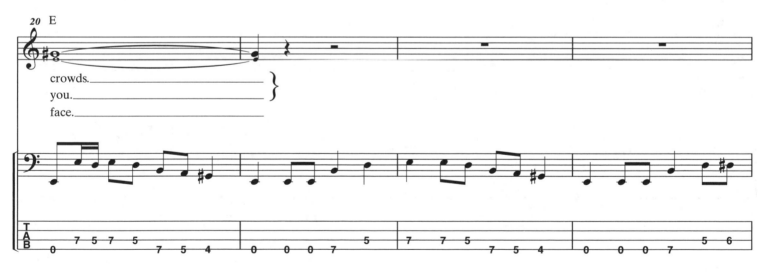

To Coda ⊕

Dance the Night Away - 4 - 2

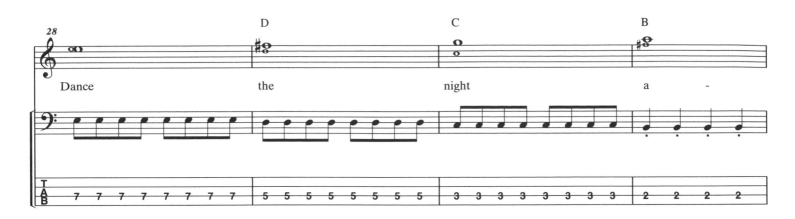

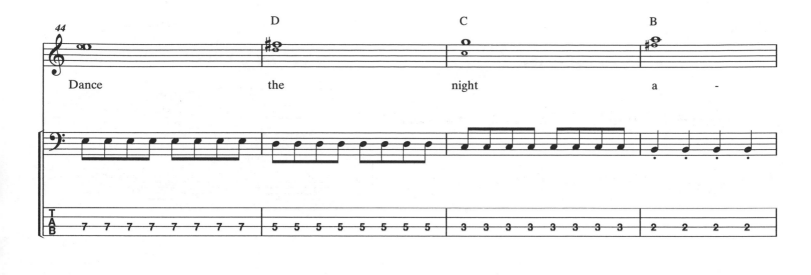

Dance the Night Away - 4 - 4

I FEEL FREE

Words and Music by
JACK BRUCE and PETE BROWN

Moderately fast ♩ = 184

14

To Coda ⊕

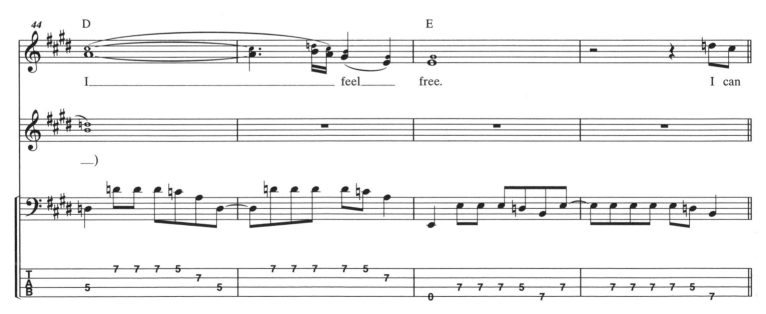

Bridge 1:

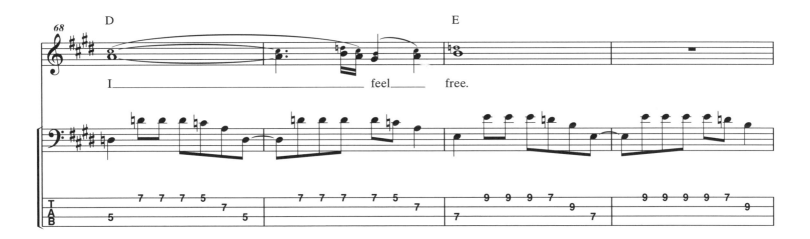

Bridge 2:

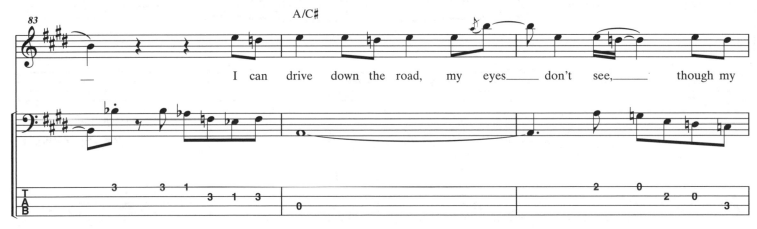

D.S. % al Coda

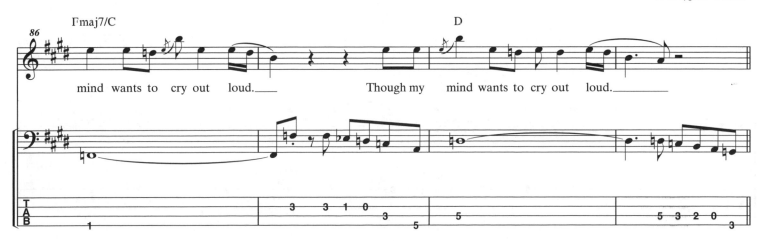

⊕ *Coda*   *Outro:*

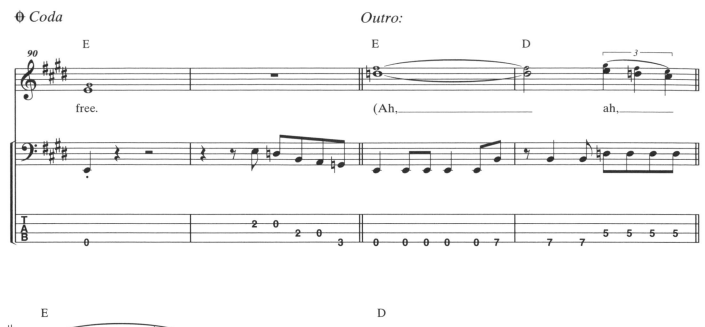

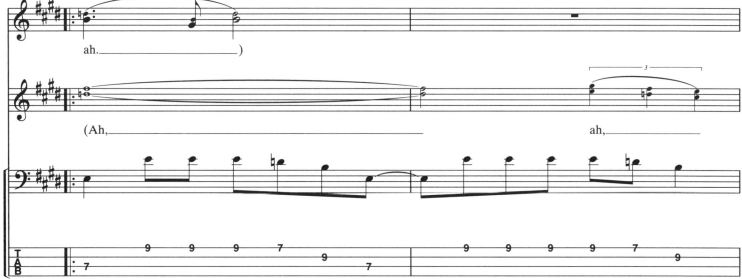

Repeat and fade

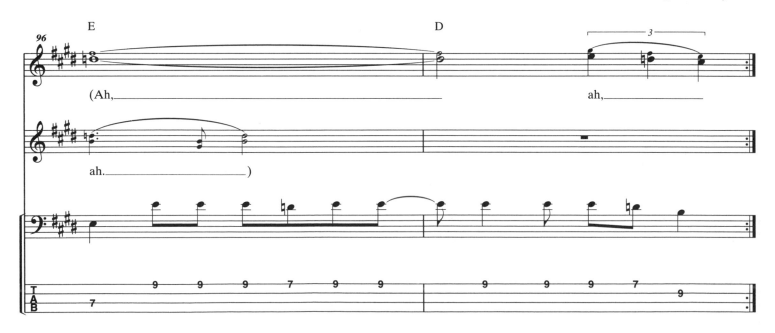

I'M SO GLAD

Words and Music by
SKIP JAMES

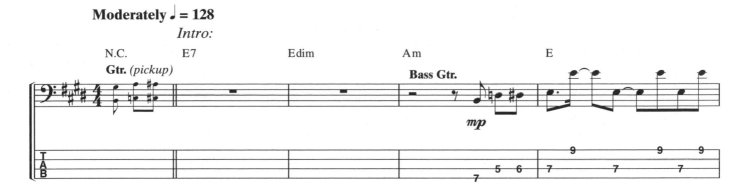

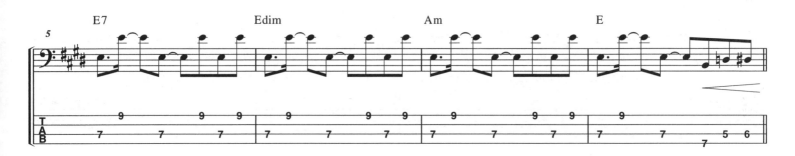

I'm So Glad - 7 - 1

Verse 1:

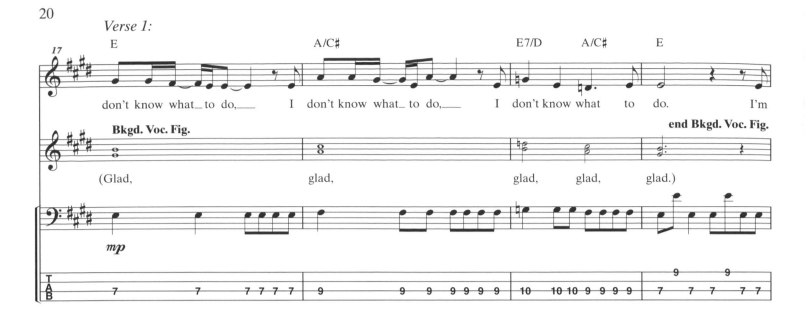

don't know what_ to do,___ I don't know what_ to do,___ I don't know what to do. I'm

(Glad, glad, glad, glad, glad.)

w/Bkgd. Voc. Fig.

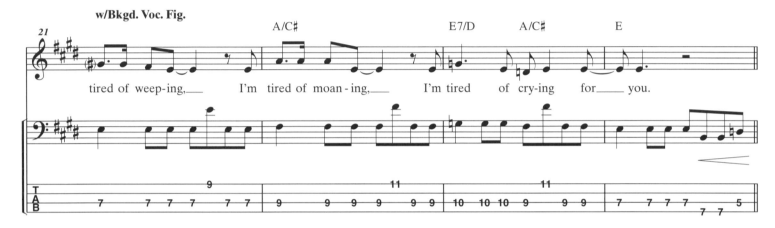

tired of weep-ing,___ I'm tired of moan-ing,___ I'm tired of cry-ing for___ you.

Chorus:

I'm_ so glad, I'm_ so glad,___ I'm glad,___ I'm glad,___ I'm___ glad.

I'm_ so glad, I'm_ so glad,___ I'm glad,___ I'm glad,___ I'm___ glad. I'm

22

Guitar Solo:

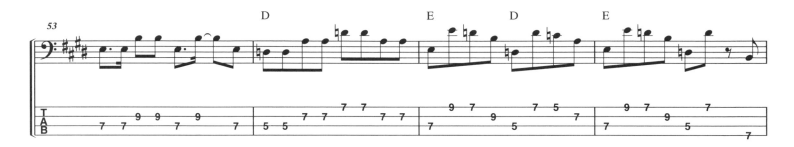

w/Bkgd. Voc. Fig., *4 times*

I'm— so glad,   I'm— so glad,—— I'm glad,—— I'm glad,—— I'm— glad.

I'm—so glad,   I'm—so glad,—— I'm glad,—— I'm glad,—— I'm— glad.

I'm—so glad,   I'm— so glad,—— I'm glad,—— I'm glad,—— I'm—glad.

I'm— so glad,   I'm— so glad,—— I'm glad,—— I'm glad,—— I'm— glad.

I'm So Glad - 7 - 6

Outro:

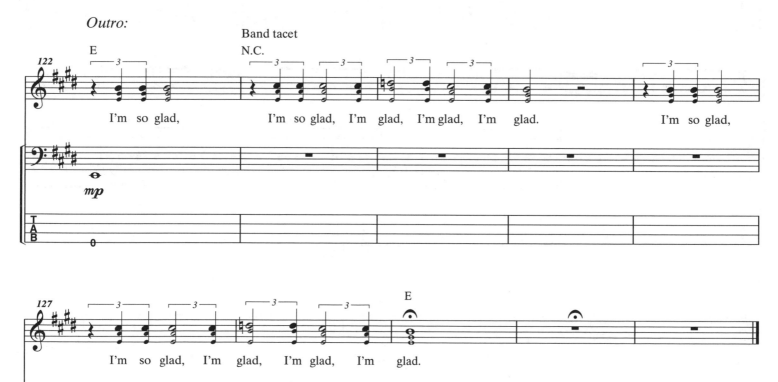

I'm So Glad - 7 - 7

NEVER TELL YOUR MOTHER SHE'S OUT OF TUNE

Words and Music by
JACK BRUCE and PETE BROWN

Moderately ♩ = 120

you shout-ing, "Hey,___ what a-bout when you___ are an old___ man?"___

To Coda ⊕

For-tun-ate-ly, ba-by, I'd___ al-read-y locked the door.___

Horns

Interlude:

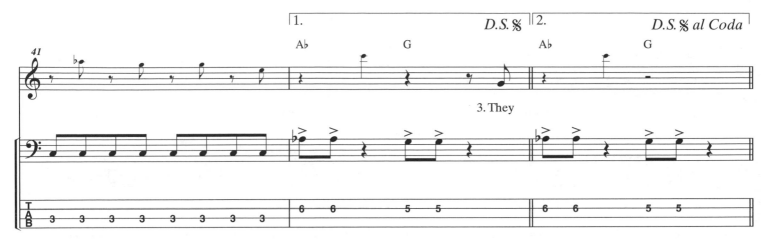

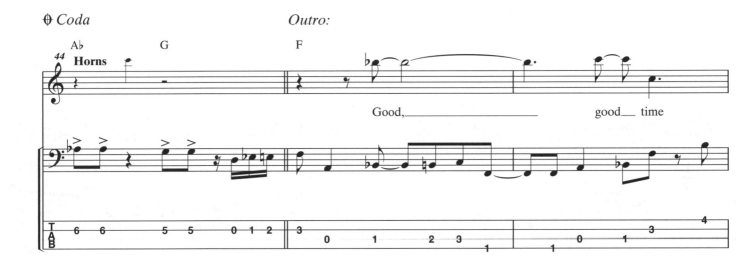

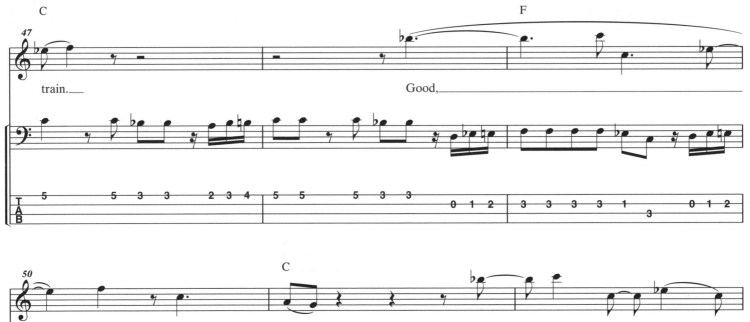

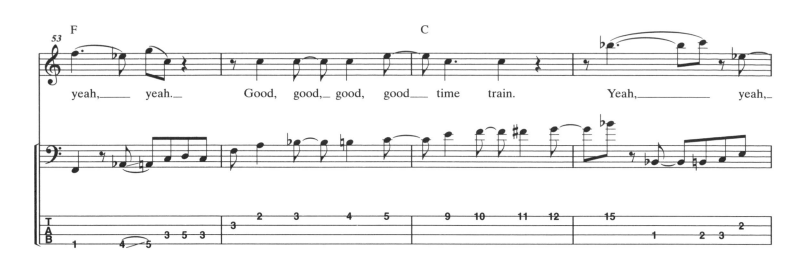

Begin fade   *Fade out*

Verse 3:
They say there are men who are blue like me in the stars.
Beards for the weird and bars for bizarre guitarmen.
Fortunately, baby, I'd already joined the force.

Verse 4:
Good time train, well, it does not need any track.
It wins the race to the place where I'm gonna pack up.
Fortunately, baby, I'd already grabbed the sky.

Verse 5:
Instrumental

Verse 6:
All the days that the road has spent on me;
Judges shout you must slave to be a freeman.
Fortunately, baby, I ain't never coming back.

N.S.U.

Words and Music by
JACK BRUCE

32

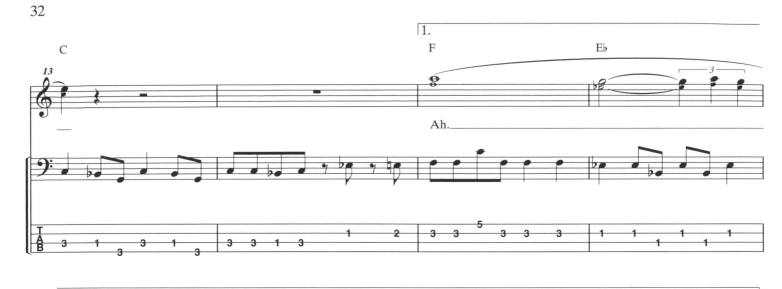

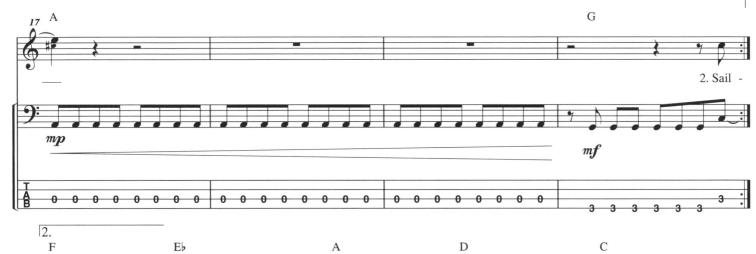

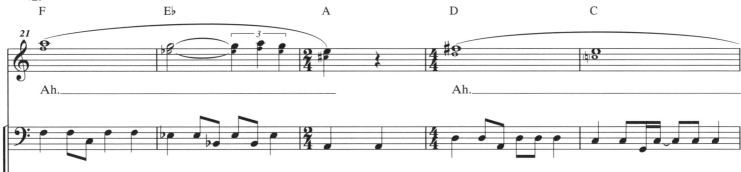

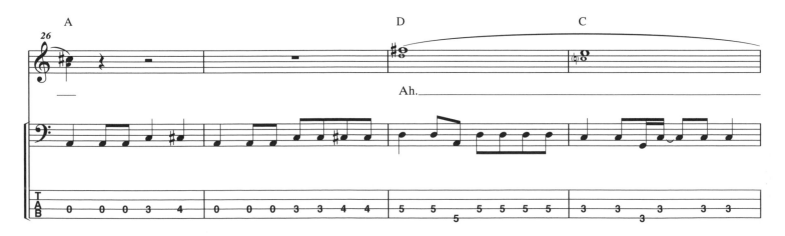

N.S.U. - 5 - 2

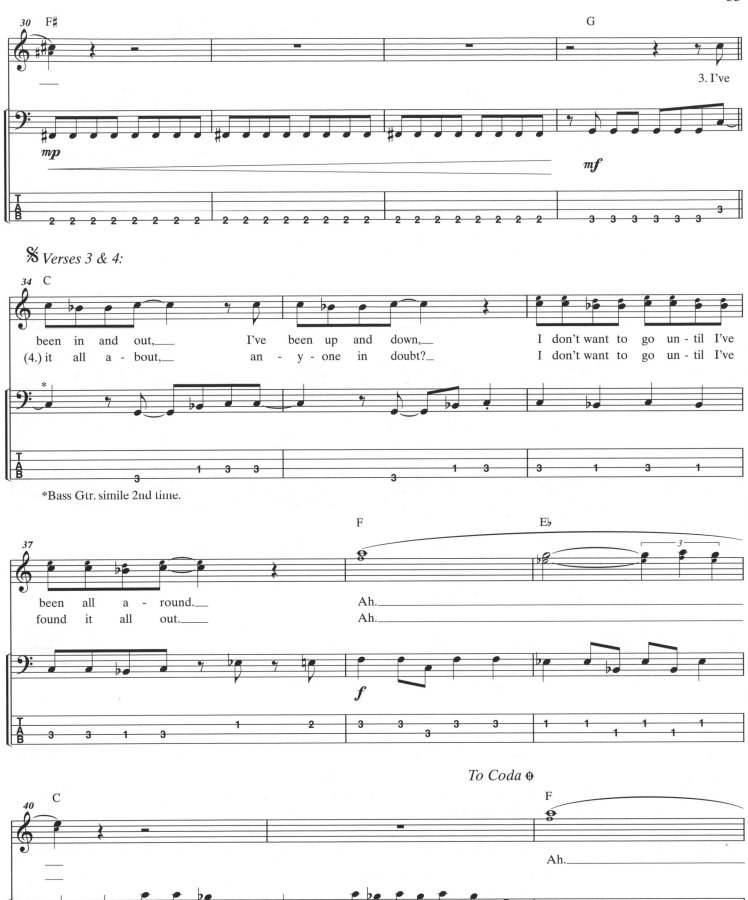

%% *Verses 3 & 4:*

been in and out,___ I've been up and down,___ I don't want to go un - til I've
(4.) it all a - bout,___ an - y - one in doubt?___ I don't want to go un - til I've

*Bass Gtr. simile 2nd time.

been all a - round.___ Ah.___
found it all out.___ Ah.___

To Coda

Ah.___

34

Guitar Solo:

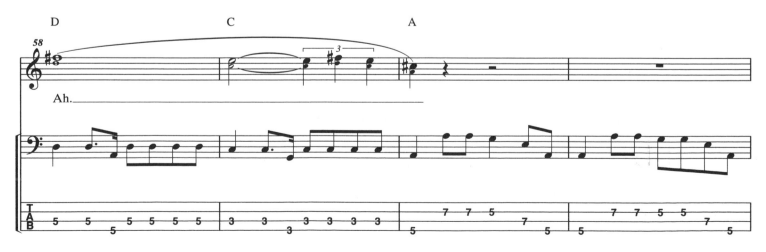

D.S. 𝄋 al Coda

4. What's

Coda

POLITICIAN

Words and Music by
JACK BRUCE and PETE BROWN

*Bass Gtr. simile on repeats.

To Coda ⊕

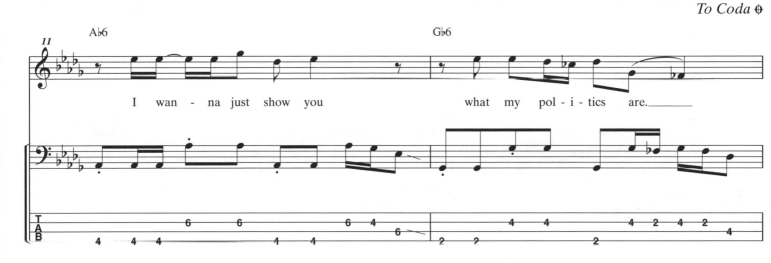

I wan - na just show you   what my pol - i - tics are.____

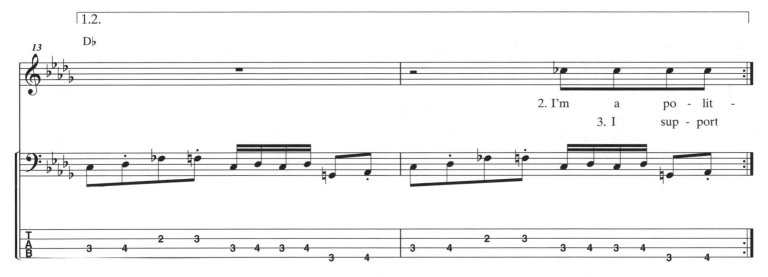

1.2.

2. I'm   a   po - lit -
3. I   sup - port

3.

Guitar Solo:

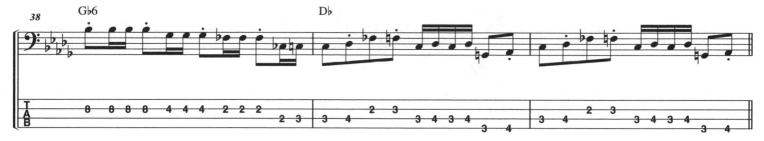

D.S. %. al Coda

Coda

Outro:　　　　　　　　　*Begin fade*　　　　　　　　　　　*Fade out*

Mm,_____　　　　　　mm,　　　mm.____

Verse 2:
I'm a political man,
And I practice what I preach.
I'm a political man,
And I practice what I preach.
So don't deny me, baby,
Not while you're in my reach.

Verse 3:
I support the left,
Though I'm leaning, leaning to the right.
I support the left,
Though I'm leaning to the right.
But I'm just not there
When it's coming to a fight.
(To Guitar Solo:)

ROPE LADDER TO THE MOON

Words and Music by
JACK BRUCE and PETE BROWN

Moderately ♩ = 88

Intro:

Verse 2:

asked me to a meet-ing in a cot-tage in the snow.___ You gave me cen-tral heat-ing,___ I

can't for-get the glow.___ You asked me to a week-end

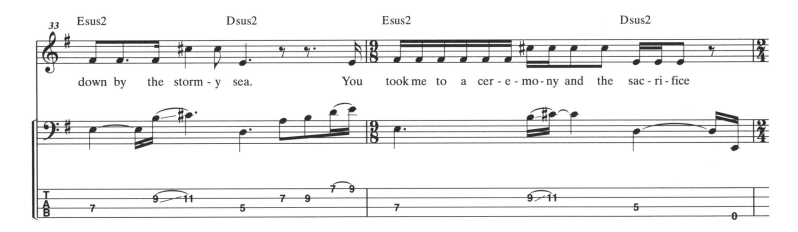

down by the storm-y sea. You took me to a cer-e-mo-ny and the sac-ri-fice

was me,

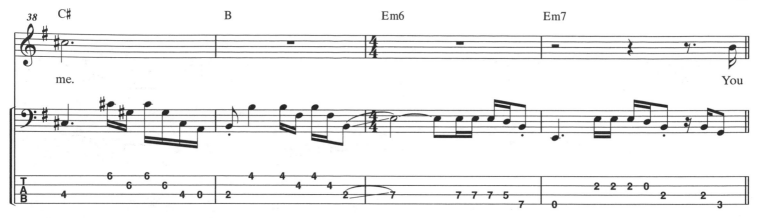

Verse 3:

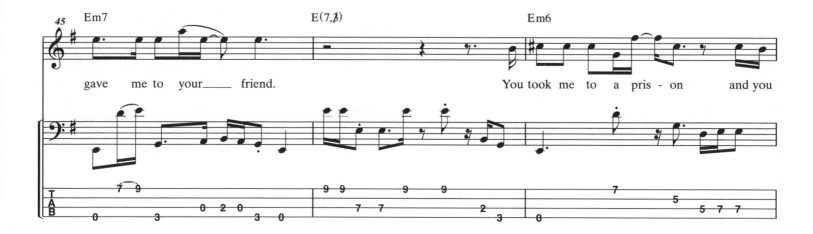

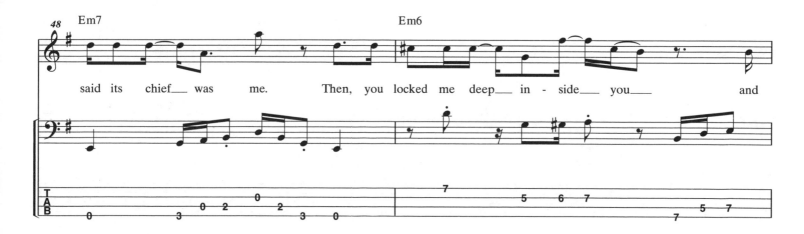

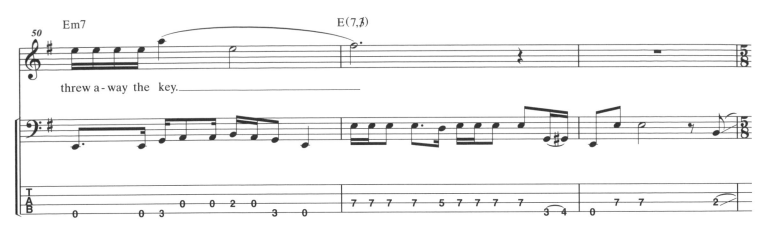

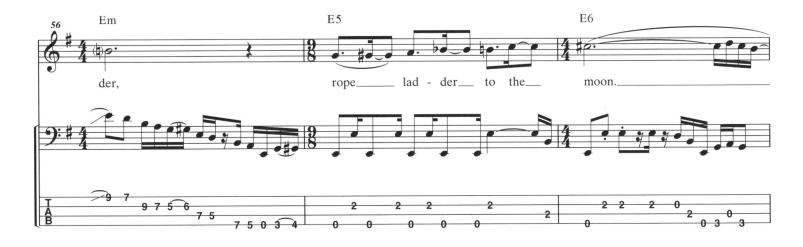

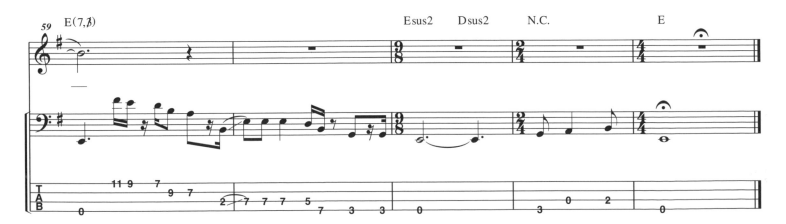

THEME FOR AN IMAGINARY WESTERN

Words and Music by
JACK BRUCE and PETE BROWN

*Chords played on piano.

*Bass Gtr. simile on repeat.

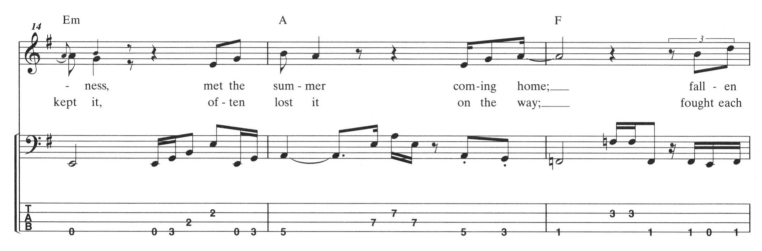

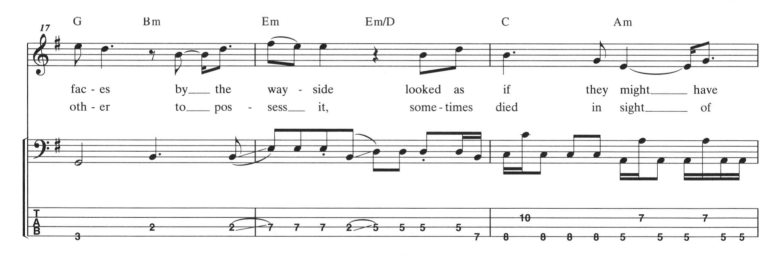

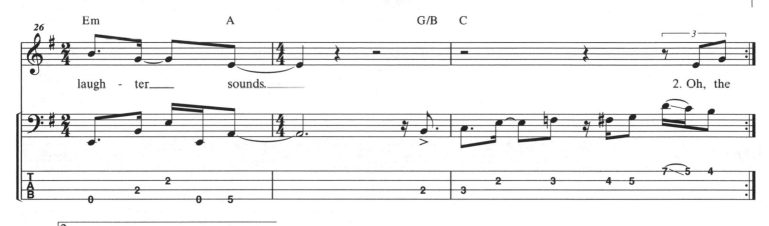

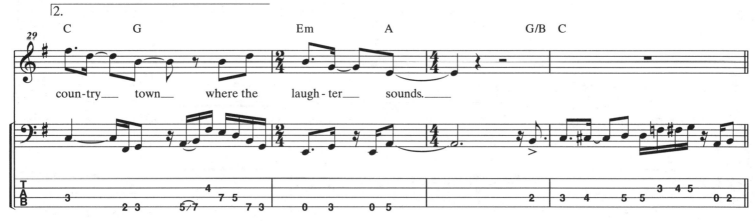

Outro:

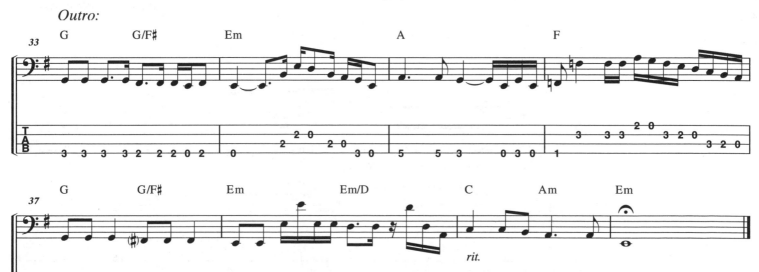

SUNSHINE OF YOUR LOVE

Words and Music by
JACK BRUCE, PETE BROWN
and ERIC CLAPTON

Moderately ♩ = 112

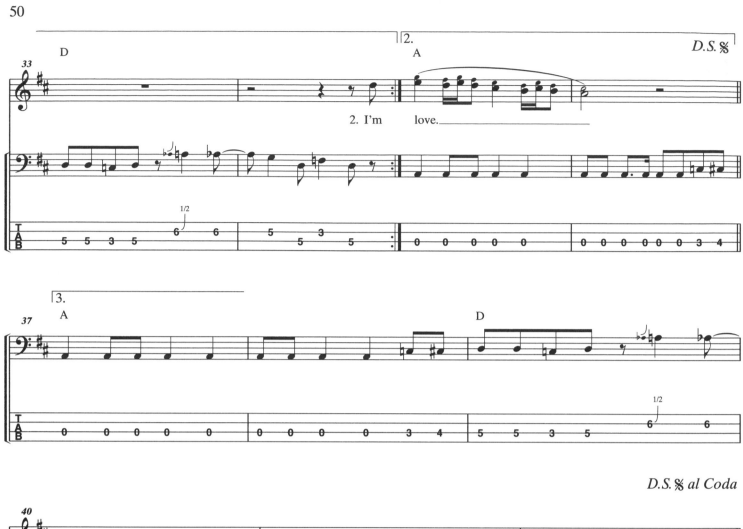

2. I'm   love._____

D.S. 𝄋 al Coda

4. I'm

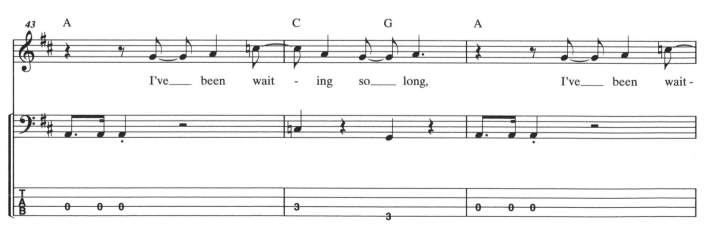

✛ *Coda*

I've___ been wait - ing so___ long,   I've___ been wait-

-ing___ so___ long,___ I've___ been wait - ing so___ long,

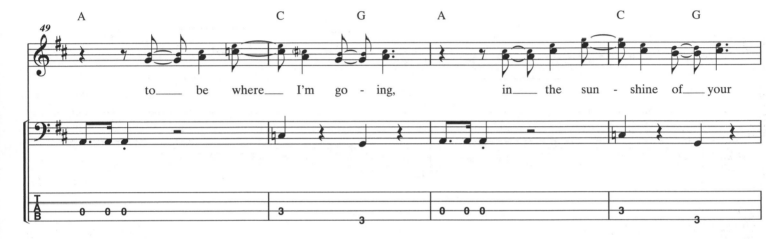

to___ be where___ I'm go - ing, in___ the sun - shine of___ your

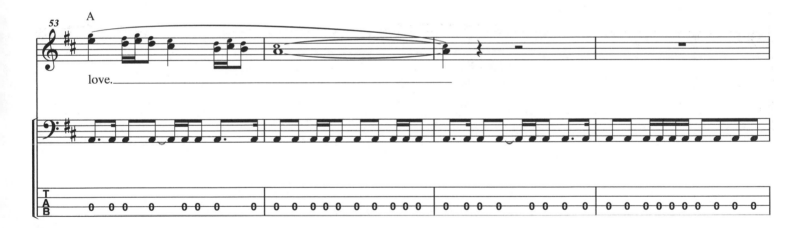

love.___

Begin fade *Fade out*

SWLABR

Words and Music by
JACK BRUCE and PETE BROWN

Moderately ♩ = 126

Intro:

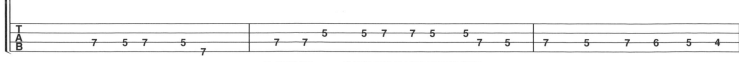

1. Com - ing to me in the morn - ing, leav - ing me at night.
2. Run - ning to me a - cry - in', when he throws you out.
(3.) man - y fan - tas - tic col - ors, I feel in a won - der land.

Com - ing to me in the morn - ing,
Run - ning to me a cry - in',
Man - y fan - tas - tic col - ors,

To Coda ⊕

leav - ing me a - lone.
on your own a - gain.
makes me feel so good.

You've got that

SWLABR - 4 - 1

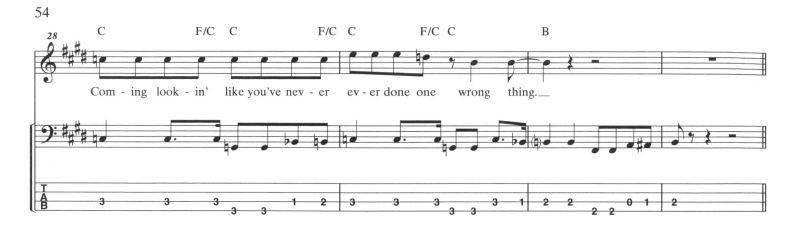

Com - ing look - in' like you've nev - er ev - er done one wrong thing.___

Guitar Solo:

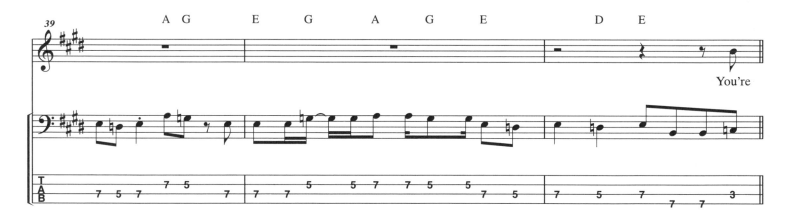

You're

Bridge 2:

com - in' to me___ with that soul - ful_ look on your face._____ You're

WE'RE GOING WRONG

Words and Music by
JACK BRUCE

To Coda ⊕

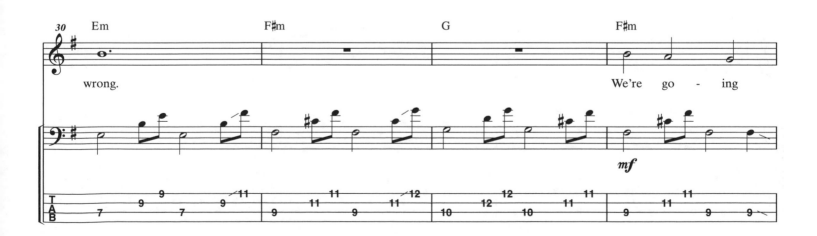

We're Going Wrong - 4 - 2

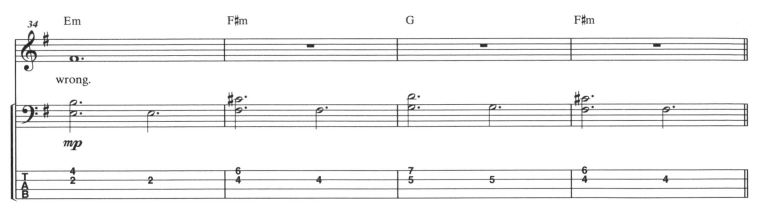

◐ *Coda*

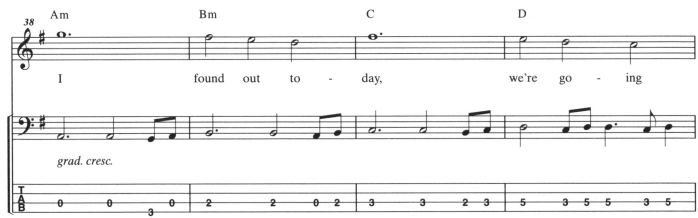

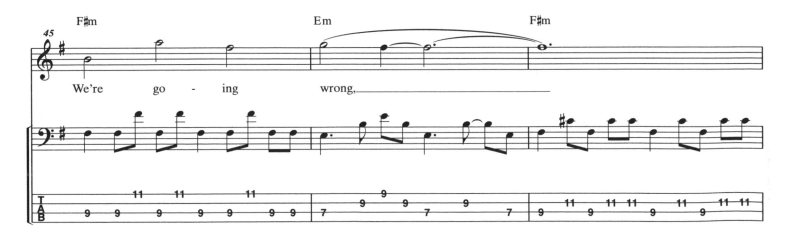

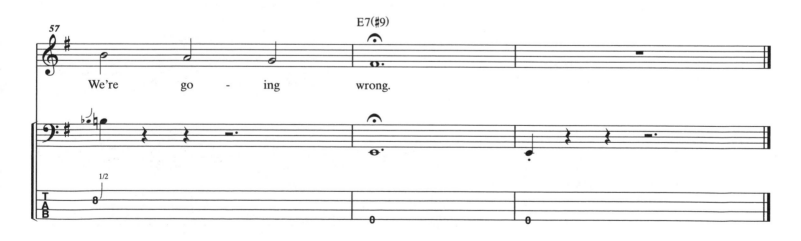

We're Going Wrong - 4 - 4

WHITE ROOM

Words and Music by
JACK BRUCE and PETE BROWN

*Bass Gtr. simile on repeats.

White Room - 5 - 1

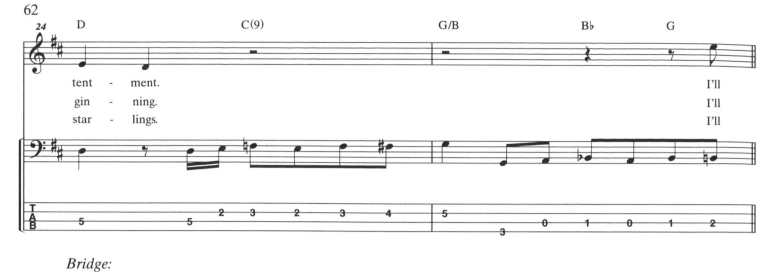

Bridge:

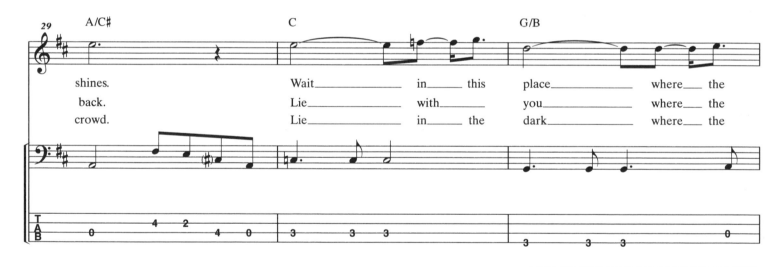

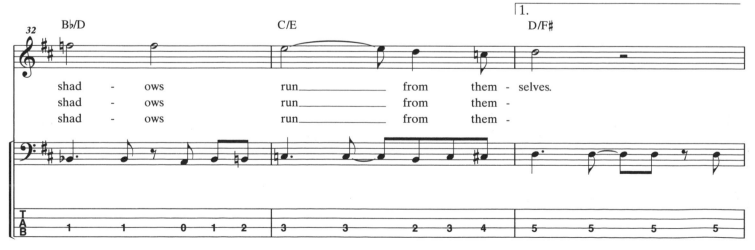

White Room - 5 - 3

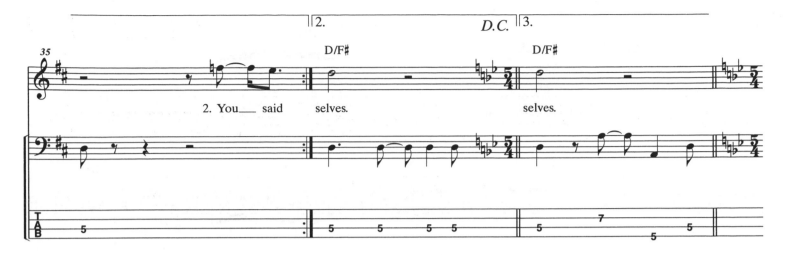

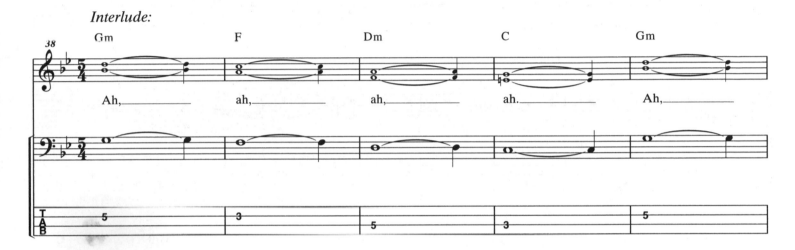

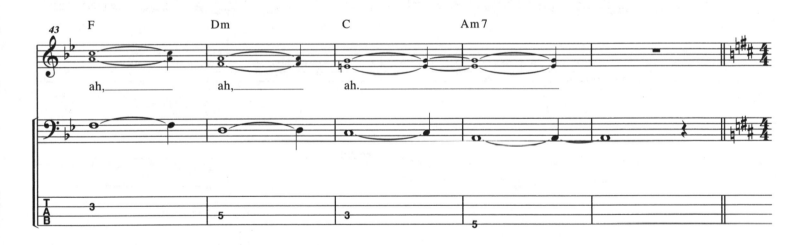

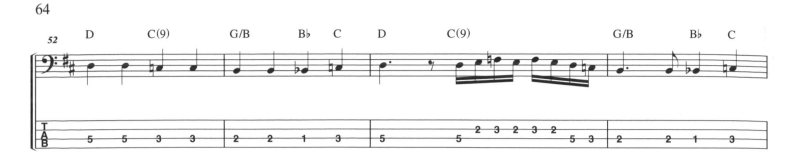

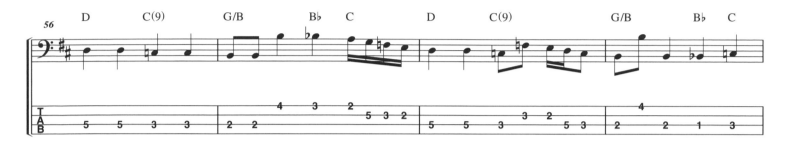

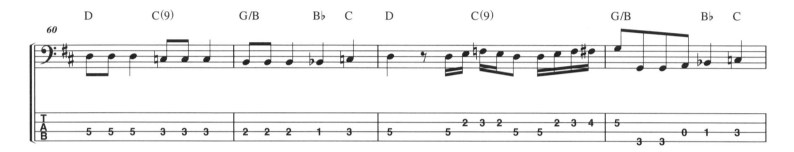

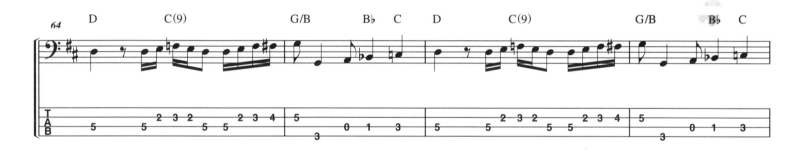

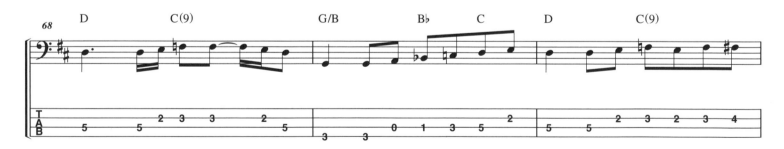

Begin fade

Fade out

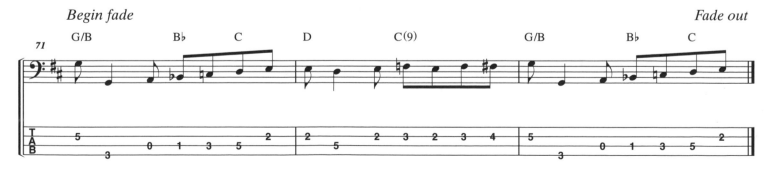